D1071634

GABRA

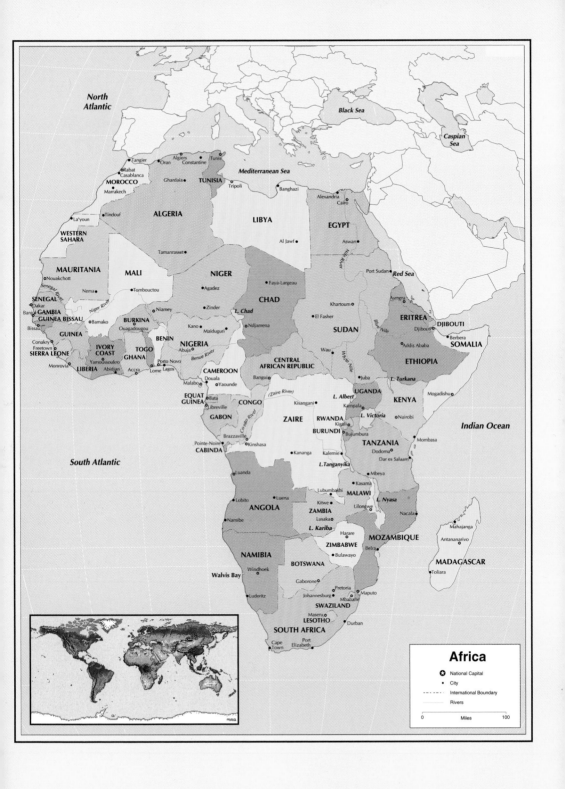

North
Atlantic

Black Sea

Caspian
Sea

Tangier
Rabat
Casablanca
Marrakech
MOROCCO

Algiers
Oran Constantine
Tunis
TUNISIA
Ghardaia

Mediterranean Sea

Tripoli

Banghazi

Alexandria
Cairo

La'youn Tindouf

WESTERN
SAHARA

ALGERIA

LIBYA

EGYPT

Al Jawf

Aswan

Tamanrasset

Nile River

MAURITANIA

Nouakchott

MALI

NIGER

Fayá-Largeau

Port Sudan
Red Sea

Nema

Tombouctou

Agadez

CHAD

Asmera

Niger River

Zinder

L. Chad

Khartoum

ERITREA

DJIBOUTI

SENEGAL
Dakar
GAMBIA
Banjul
GUINEA BISSAU
Bissau

Niamey

Kano

Ndjamena

El Fasher

Blue Nile

Djibouti
Berbera

Bamako

BURKINA

Maiduguri

SOMALIA

Conakry
Freetown
SIERRA LEONE

GUINEA

Ouagadougou

BENIN

NIGERIA

Abuja

Wau

SUDAN

White Nile

Addis Ababa

ETHIOPIA

Monrovia

IVORY
COAST
Yamoussoukro
LIBERIA Abidjan

TOGO
GHANA

Accra

Porto Novo
Lome Lagos

Benue River

CENTRAL
AFRICAN REPUBLIC

Bangui

Juba

L. Turkana

CAMEROON

Douala
Malabo
Yaounde

Mogadishu

EQUAT.
GUINEA
Bata

Libreville

CONGO

(Zaire River)

Kisangani

UGANDA

L. Albert

Kampala

KENYA

Indian Ocean

GABON

Congo River

ZAIRE

RWANDA
Kigali
BURUNDI
Bujumbura

L. Victoria

Nairobi

Pointe-Noire
CABINDA

Brazzaville
Kinshasa

Kananga

Kalemie

TANZANIA

Dodoma

Mombasa

South Atlantic

Luanda

L.Tanganyika

Dar es Salaam

Lobito
Luena

Lubumbashi

Mbeya

Kasama

Kitwe

MALAWI

L. Nyasa

ANGOLA

ZAMBIA

Lilongwe

Nacala

Namibe

Lusaka

L. Kariba

Harare

MOZAMBIQUE

Mahajanga

NAMIBIA

ZIMBABWE

Antananarivo

Bulawayo

Beira

MADAGASCAR

BOTSWANA

Windhoek

Walvis Bay

Gaborone

Pretoria

Maputo

Toliara

Luderitz

Johannesburg
Mbabane

SWAZILAND

Maseru
LESOTHO

Cape
Town

Port
Elizabeth

Durban

SOUTH AFRICA

Africa

⬟ National Capital
• City
-·-·- International Boundary
― Rivers

0   Miles   100

The Heritage Library of African Peoples

GABRA

Aneesa Kassam, Ph.D.

THE ROSEN PUBLISHING GROUP, INC.
NEW YORK

Published in 1995 by The Rosen Publishing Group, Inc.
29 East 21st Street, New York, NY 10010

First Edition

Manufactured in the United States of America

Library of Congress Cataloging-in-Publication Data

Kassam, Aneesa.
    Gabra / Aneesa Kassam — 1st ed.
      p. cm. — (The heritage library of African peoples)
    Includes bibliographical references and index.
    ISBN 0-8239-1760-6
    1. Gabbra (African people)—History—Juvenile literature.
2. Gabbra (African people)—Social life and customs—Juvenile
literature. [1. Gabbra (African people)]
I. Title. II. Series.
DT433.545.G32K37   1995
967.6—dc20   94-45817
                                                      CIP
                                                      AC

Contents

Introduction 6

1. The Gabra People 9

2. The Land and Pastoral
   Economy 12

3. Social and Political
   Organization 20

4. The Gabra Concept of Time 39

5. Social Change and
   Development 45

Glossary 59

For Further Reading 61

Index 63

INTRODUCTION

THERE IS EVERY REASON FOR US TO KNOW something about Africa and to understand its past and the way of life of its peoples. Africa is a rich continent that has for centuries provided the world with art, culture, labor, wealth, and natural resources. It has vast mineral deposits, fossil fuels, and commercial crops.

But perhaps most important is the fact that fossil evidence indicates that human beings originated in Africa. The earliest traces of human beings and their tools are almost two million years old. Their descendants have migrated throughout the world. To be human is to be of African descent.

The experiences of the peoples who stayed in Africa are as rich and as diverse as of those who established themselves elsewhere. This series of books describes their environment, their modes of subsistence, their relationships, and their customs and beliefs. The books present the variety of languages, histories, cultures, and religions that are to be found on the African continent. They demonstrate the historical linkages between African peoples and the way contemporary Africa has been affected by European colonial rule.

Africa is large, complex, and diverse. It encompasses an area of more than 11,700,000 square miles. The United States, Europe, and India could fit easily into it. The sheer size is an indication of the continent's great variety in geography, terrain, climate, flora, fauna, peoples, languages, and cultures.

Much of contemporary Africa has been shaped by European colonial rule, industrialization, urbanization, and the demands of a world economic system. For more than seventy years, large regions of Africa were ruled by Great Britain, France, Belgium, Portugal, and Spain. African peoples from various ethnic, linguistic, and cultural backgrounds were brought together to form colonial states.

For decades Africans struggled to gain their independence. It was not until after World War II that the colonial territories become independent African states. Today, almost all of Africa is ruled by Africans. Large numbers of Africans live in modern cities. Rural Africa is also being transformed, and yet its people still engage in many of their age-old customs and beliefs.

Contemporary circumstances and natural events have not always been kind to ordinary Africans. Today, however, new popular social movements and technological innovations pose great promise for future development.

George C. Bond, Ph.D., Director
Institute of African Studies
Columbia University, New York

The Gabra live in the arid regions of Ethiopia, Kenya, and Somalia in East Africa.

chapter

1

THE GABRA PEOPLE

THE GABRA ARE NOMADIC CAMEL-HERDERS who live in the hot, dry regions of southern Ethiopia, northern Kenya, and Somalia in East and Northeast Africa. These people have a long history, but they have not always been known as the Gabra. Before Great Britain colonized East Africa, the Gabra and many other ethnic groups belonged to a wider nation known as the Oromo.

The Oromo are one of the most populous peoples of the Horn of Africa, numbering some 25 to 30 million. They live in a territory stretching from the borders of Tigray in Ethiopia in the north to the Indian Ocean in Kenya in the south. Their former land is now divided among three countries: Ethiopia, where the Oromo are the major ethnic group; Somalia, where they are related to the majority Hawiyya group; and Kenya, where they are represented by a number of groups such as the Booran, Gabra, Waata, Orma, Garri, and Sakuyye.

Across this vast territory, all these groups share the Oromo language, which belongs to the Afro-Asiatic language group. Oromo is a member of a subgroup called Eastern Cushitic, languages that are widely spoken in the countries of the Horn of Africa. The Kushites, the ancient people from whom this language is derived, are believed to be the ancestors of the Oromo. Some three thousand years ago, the Kushitic empire stretched from India to Africa. Many aspects of this civilization are still present in the Oromo culture. The Oromo calendar and method of measuring time are inherited from this remote past. The system of recording time, *ayyaana*, is used to structure all of Oromo society.

Before the colonial period, the present-day Gabra made up one of the southernmost Oromo divisions. The British established political boundaries between Ethiopia and Kenya, disregarding the traditional Oromo territorial boundaries. Two parts of a single Oromo division were split from each other by this new boundary.

Today the Gabra are found on both sides of the Kenya-Ethiopia border. In Kenya, the majority occupy an area of about 15,400 square miles in the Marsabit District of Eastern Province. This territory was demarcated by the Brit-

ETHIOPIA

MEGADO ESCARPMENT

Sodo • • Wendo

SUDAN

SIDAMO PROVINCE

Ganale R.

Dawa R.

Webi Gestra R.

Lake Turkana

Mega Woreda District

Dolo

North Horr

GABRA • Moyale

Mandera •

Lodwar •

SOMALIA

Turkwel R.

Chalbi Desert

Marsabit District

El Wak •

KENYA

Wajir •

Lake Baringo

Waso Nyiro R.

Indian Ocean

UGANDA

Isiolo District

EASTERN PROVINCE

Lake Victoria

• Nairobi

AFRICA (ETHIOPIA) (KENYA)

TANZANIA

Gabraland

ish colonial government at the beginning of the century. It is bordered by Lake Turkana to the west, the Bule Deera Plains to the east, the Megado Escarpment to the north, and the Chalbi Desert to the south. A small community of Gabra live along the Waso Nyiro River in the Isiolo District of Kenya. The Gabra in Kenya currently number about 50,000. About 12,500 live on the Ethiopian side, in the Mega Woreda District of Sidamo Province.

For the Gabra, like the Booran, this territory is a kind of no-man's-land between two countries, in which they move back and forth with their herds of cattle, camels, sheep, and goats. ▲

chapter

2

THE LAND AND PASTORAL ECONOMY

LIKE ALL OROMO, THE GABRA USE A COMPLEX
system for classifying the land in which they live.
They divide it into two major zones, the *badda*,
or highlands, and the *gammojji*, or lowlands.
In the *badda* the climate is cool and wet. The
vegetation is rich and varied. Water that collects
in open pans, crevices, and ponds can be used
in the dry season. The ground is fairly even, and
grass-covered plains are fringed with woods and
forests. It is here that cattle, including oxen,
thrive. The *gammojji*, on the other hand, are hot
and dry areas that border the desert. Rainfall is
scant, and vegetation is sparse. Plants contain a
high amount of salt because of the nature of the
soil. Trees and bushes are armed with thick and
prickly thorns to retain moisture. Water must be
obtained from deep wells. The terrain is difficult,
either scattered with huge volcanic boulders or
completely barren and sandy. In the wet season,

The *Adenium obesum,* "rose of the desert," is a beautiful, brightly colored, but poisonous tree.

however, the desert comes to life with flowers and nutritious herbs and grasses. It is here that camels and small stock like sheep and goats thrive.

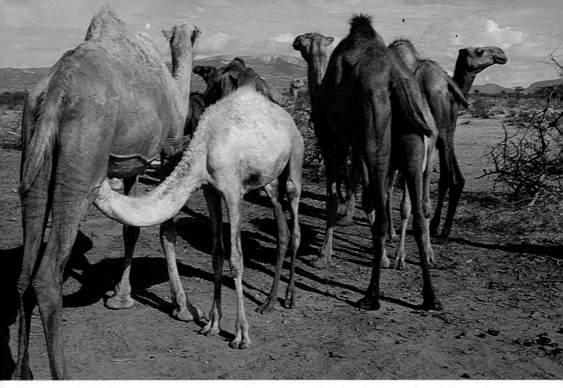

The Gabra are experts in camel breeding. The first few months of the life of a camel are very difficult. This young camel is nursing.

The Gabra must move as the seasons change to find water and grazing land for their animals. During the wet season they move into the highland areas of their habitat in Ethiopia and Kenya, such as the Hurri Hills in the center and the Megado Escarpment to the north. In the dry season they move slowly back into the Kenyan lowlands bordering the Chalbi Desert, to replenish the salt in the diet of their animals and to use the water stored in the wells.

Through these seasonal movements, they allow the land to "rest," to recover through natural regeneration from the impact made by humans and animals. The Gabra were always highly concerned with environmental matters.

The land, the source of food and life, was safe-guarded through customary laws and traditions.

▼ THE LIVESTOCK ▼

Since the various categories of livestock—cattle, camels, sheep, and goats—feed on different types of plants and have varying needs for water, they are divided into herds and sent into separate parts of the territory. Cattle, for instance, do not thrive in the intense heat and rocky terrain of the lowlands. They are kept at higher elevations where the ground is more even and where they can be watered at least every third day. Because cattle are somewhat difficult to maintain and easily killed by drought, Gabra own relatively few herds of cattle today. Milk is the main food of the Gabra. The categories of livestock they own are known as the "three with sweet milk": cattle, camels, and small stock (sheep and goats).

Camels are the mainstay of the Gabra pastoral economy. They are hardy animals that can survive in extreme conditions with little water and still provide a family with adequate milk, even in the dry season. Through centuries of their coexistence with these animals, the Gabra have evolved a camel "culture," which they share with other Eastern Cushitic camel peoples such as the Rendille and Somali. These groups are known as the Warra Gaallaa, or "people of the

Camels are essential for the survival of the Gabra. Camels are hardy animals that provide milk even during the dry season. They are also used to transport water from wells and to carry the belongings of a family when it moves from one location to another.

camel." Camels are also used as pack animals, to carry water from the wells, and to move the belongings of the family when they migrate from one seasonal pasture to another. The Gabra live in collapsible huts, dome-shaped houses made of skins and hides and mats woven of a fiber called sisal.

The large herds of sheep and goats also do well in the lowlands, where there are fewer ticks and more salty vegetation that the animals like. Goats and sheep need water only every five to six days. Their meat can also be used as food, especially during the dry season when milk supplies are low. Small stock are the "money" of the Gabra. They trade the animals for other food items such as tea, sugar, and grain products as well as manufactured goods like kerosene lamps, torches, batteries, and aluminum cooking pots. Goats are also used to barter for services like those of the blacksmith or to pay fines in the court of law.

To avoid pressure on water and vegetation supplies near the human settlements, these different types of animals are further split into a "wet" herd and a "dry" herd. The wet herd consists of animals that have recently given birth to young and bear milk. The milk is needed to feed the family, especially young children, and the herd is kept close to the settlements where the head of the family and his wife or wives live.

This herd is known as the *warra* herd, after the Oromo word for "family" or "home." The dry herds consist of animals that are not providing milk. These herds, known as *fora* herds, are sent to remote areas of Gabraland under the supervision of young male herders and a few elders. Conditions in the *fora* satellite camps are harsh. They serve as a place where young boys learn to survive in a hostile environment in preparation for the difficult life ahead of them.

▼ MIGRATIONS ▼

The main or base camp of the Gabra also moves according to a seasonal pattern. Within these major migrations, smaller moves are made for many reasons. These include short-distance shifts every six to eight weeks to avoid the accumulation of ticks and dung in the settlement, and larger shifts, which are made to "follow the rain." Rainfall is very localized in Gabraland, and scouts are sent out to survey the territory and to bring back news about the pastures and the availability of water. If the prospects are good, the scouts return signifying joyful tidings by flowers stuck in the tufts of their hair.

Camps are made up of one or more families. Everyone must cooperate to look after the different types of livestock spread all over Gabra territory. The work of watering the animals is arduous and difficult, especially in the lowlands,

Gabra camps usually consist of several families. All of the families are responsible for the care of the livestock.

where the water must be drawn up from wells. The wells are often as much as 100 to 130 feet deep, and it takes a human chain of four or more to bring up the water. To create a rhythm that will keep the workers moving, the herders sing as they work. Because of this, the wells of Gabra and Booranland are known as the "singing wells."

In order to survive in this harsh environment and to perform all the tasks related to the care of the animals, the Gabra must cooperate in every project. This is achieved through their social organization.▲

chapter

3

SOCIAL AND POLITICAL ORGANIZATION

THE NAME GABRA (OR GABARO) DID NOT originally designate a distinct people. It stood for a concept in the Oromo system of thought.

The Oromo system of classification was derived from the figure of the human body and plainly expressed states that everything in the universe has two distinct but related parts. The human body is divided into two by the trunk. It has five limbs: a head, two arms, and two legs. The two hands and two feet subdivide into five fingers and five toes; the head has two eyes and two ears, and so forth. This system was used as a model to classify society and to place everything in the universe in time and in space.

Like the human body, the Oromo nation was divided into two halves, known as the Booran and the Barrentu. Booran was the name of the eldest son of the founder of the Oromo people,

The Gabra belong to the Oromo people.

Horo. The name (H)Oromo (the letter H is not always pronounced in Oromo) is derived from the name of this ancestor. The name of the second son was Barrentu. Booran married three wives who bore him three sons. Barrentu married two wives who bore him two sons. These sons founded the five territories of Oromoland, which together constituted the five limbs of the Oromo social body. Each of the five groups is divided into paired halves called moieties. The pairs are the Raayaa and the Assebu; the

21

Machaa and the Tulamaa; the Sabbo and the
Goonaa; the Sikko and the Mando, and the Ittu
and the Humbana. Dividing the five groups into
moieties represented the right-hand and left-
hand sides of each founding son. The sides also
corresponded to the directions of east and west.

Just as the right hand is usually the stronger,
so the right-hand division of each group was
considered the "senior" moiety, and the weaker
or left-hand side was considered the "junior"
moiety. The division formed first was the
right-hand one. This system was also true in
individual families: The first-born son was considered stronger than his younger male siblings.
This was known as the Booran/Gabaro relationship. The idea of Booranahood represented the
principle of seniority in society, while that of
Gabarohood stood for the principle of juniority.
The name Gabra is derived from this principle.

▼ SENIORITY AND JUNIORITY ▼

Since there can be only one first-born son but
many other sons in a family, the whole of society
can be seen as composed of the first-born sons
and their younger male siblings. This concept is
reflected in the Oromo saying: "Nine are the
Booran and ninety are the Gabaro." In traditional Oromo society, only male children were
taken into account in this division of society.

This principle of juniority and seniority was

From birth, the eldest son is groomed for the responsibility of replacing his father as head of the family.

very important. It was used to express a number of economic, social, and political relationships among the members of society.

At the death of his father, the first-born son inherited the estate and took charge of managing the family property, either farmland or domestic animals. From the time of his birth, the eldest son was trained for the responsibility of replacing his father as head of the family. He therefore occupied a privileged position. Eldest sons were also groomed to take political leadership in the Oromo system of government, known as *Gada*. By virtue of being the first-born, the Booran were therefore the rulers, and the Gabaro or younger sons belonged to those who were ruled. This hierarchical relationship was a source of potential conflict that Oromo society sought to control with a system of checks and balances.

The Oromo believed that each side of the divided whole was necessary and vital to the existence of the other. To express this, the Oromo say that to wash one's hands, both hands must be used; one hand cannot wash without the help of the other. This notion was symbolically expressed in the roles of the male and the female. Although the father was dominant in the public interest of the household, the mother was most important to domestic and ritual duties. The children followed the duality of their parents. The eldest son was associated with the political authority of the father; the youngest son was associated with the ritual authority of the mother. Similarly, at the level of society, no government could be formed without the representation of both human and spiritual authorities.

▼ METHOD OF LEADERSHIP ▼

There were five regional *Gada* assemblies representing the five territorial divisions of the

Oromo. These assemblies were elected. Before they could assume office, the *Gada* statesmen made a pilgrimage to receive the blessing of the Oromo priest-king, the *Abba Muudaa*, "Father of Anointment." This blessing was given by anointing the heads of the pilgrims with butter fat. The *Qaalluu* were leaders appointed by the *Abba Muudaa* to represent the highest level of authority in the political assemblies.

According to myth, the *Abba Muudaa* came down from heaven in a mist and was found carrying a drum in which was a poisonous black snake. On his head was a black-and-white striped turban, and on his upper left arm he wore iron bracelets. The image of the drum, snake, and bracelets symbolized the power and authority of the *Qaalluu* in the political assemblies.

In the political rule of the *Gada*, the interests of the Gabaro were represented by the Booran *Qaalluu*.

▼ ECONOMIC ORGANIZATION ▼

Traditional Oromo society was also divided into three economic groups: agriculturalists (in the highlands), pastoralists (in the lowlands), and hunter-gatherers, who lived in cooperation with the two other groups. The Oromo hunter-gatherers are known as the Waata.

Whenever the Oromo settled in an area, the Booran, or elder brothers, always occupied rela-

The dress among the Gabra shows the social status of a person. The men wearing white robes and turbans and holding walking sticks are married. The hairdressing of the woman indicates that she is married and has children.

tively higher ground in comparison to the Gabaro, or younger brothers. This was done for social, political, economic, and ritual reasons as well as for defense. The Waata were considered inferior and were not allowed to live within Booran and Gabaro settlements. They occupied a position on the edges of society.

The Booran mostly farmed in the central highlands, using ox-drawn plows. They also raised some livestock, especially cattle. On the other hand, the Gabaro were herders, living a nomadic or seminomadic existence on the edge of the lowlands, but also cultivating fields when the nature of the soil permitted. The Oromo thought of high places as being close to the Creator, *Waaqa*, and it was here that the life-giving ceremonies and ritual sacrifices of live-stock were performed. The Waata also played an important role in these ceremonies.

The relationship between the elder Booran and younger Gabaro was based on this principle of balanced opposition. The Gabaro represented the mirror image of the Booran and performed opposite but equally important functions in society.

Many writers on the Oromo have misunder-stood the system of beliefs that created this balance. As a result, Gabaro have been por-trayed as conquered people who are the "sons of slaves." This was not true in traditional Oromo society, where the Gabaro formed one of the original conceptual divisions of the society.

▼ THE PRESENT-DAY GABRA ▼

Following the traditional Oromo system of classification, the people known as the Gabra people are divided into five territorial groups, called phratries. These five groups, which live in different parts of Gabraland, have their own political assemblies and administrative head-quarters or *yaa*. Each phratry has a myth of origin, which recounts how it was formed and

A Gabra elder.

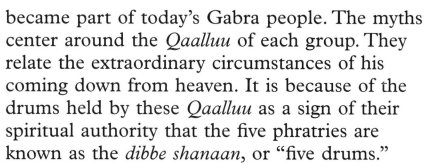

became part of today's Gabra people. The myths center around the *Qaalluu* of each group. They relate the extraordinary circumstances of his coming down from heaven. It is because of the drums held by these *Qaalluu* as a sign of their spiritual authority that the five phratries are known as the *dibbe shanaan*, or "five drums."

Several clans make up a phratry, and the clans are grouped into right-hand and left-hand moieties, as in the Oromo tradition. Clans subdivide into families descended from a common ancestor, then into groups of extended families, and lastly into nuclear families, composed of a man, his wife or wives, and their children.

Families rarely live on their own. They usually live with other families with whom they cooperate in the work of looking after the animals. These units of social organization manage the resources of the Gabra and resolve disputes.

Closely related families form a residential and herding unit known as *soloola*. The word is derived from the name for guinea fowl, which always keep close to one another as they run about looking for food. In the *soloola*, animals belonging to the extended family are kept in common enclosures.

Among the Gabra, the father heads the household unit and is known as *abba warraa*, "head of the family." He is responsible for managing the affairs of the family and of allocating duties to members. The eldest son is usually put in charge of the camel herd; the second son takes care of the goats and sheep. The sons are assisted in their herding duties by younger brothers and sisters.

The next level of residential unit is known as a *shanaaca*, derived from the word for the number five, *shanaan*. This unit is not common among the Gabra of Kenya. It is made up of more than five *soloola*. One of the family heads is appointed to represent the affairs of the whole *shanaaca* when they move into a new area. He must learn about the pasture and water resources available in the area and make arrangements to share these resources with other groups camped in the same area. He is also called upon to resolve disputes that may arise between the families.

▼ NOMADIC SETTLEMENTS ▼

The *shanaaca* is usually part of a larger kind of camp residence, known as *olla*. This is the predominant form of nomadic settlement in Gabra today. Larger *olla* are formed when security problems exist or when many members of families come together for the performance of marriage rites. The *olla* is made up of several households, either single families or *soloola*. Each unit has its own livestock enclosures but shares in the collective tasks of herding and watering

Every Gabra village has an *abba ollaa*, or village head.

Ceremonial dances are performed by the Gabra to promote *nagaya*,
or peace.

animals. A nomadic village head, known as the
abba ollaa, is appointed by all the families to
represent the settlement at the district level.
Families join an *olla* only temporarily, for a season. Then they separate to take their herds in
different directions. When an *olla* separates, its
families join settlements with other families in
their new area. The *olla* is the focus of all ceremonial activity, where rituals for peace and rain
are collectively performed and sacrifices of livestock made by each household.

Gabra women gather to dance in celebration of a successful male birth.

The *deeda*, or district, is made up of several neighboring *olla*. The heads of the *olla* appoint an *abba deedaa* who heads the district committee on which they will be represented. The *abba deedaa* has overall charge of managing the resources of that district. This includes forming

well committees to be sure all of the member
olla have a fair share of the water resources.
The herd owners take their stock to the wells in
the area on the days assigned to them by the
committee. Anyone found watering his family's
animals out of turn is punished and assessed a
fine in the form of livestock. The cleanliness and
state of repair of the well-troughs in which water
is poured for the animals to drink is also maintained and organized by the well committee.

The heads of the nomadic settlements are
responsible for organizing ceremonial activities.
The elders meet under the shade of a big tree to
discuss these and other affairs relating to the
settlements.

In the past, each territory was responsible
for its own defense in the event of a major
crisis such as a raid by a neighboring pastoral
people such as the Rendille, Somali, Samburu,
Dassenatch, or Turkana. A special assembly
met to form a militia to protect the community,
the communal resources, and the livestock of
individual herd owners and their families.

This was done in conjunction with the
elected political leaders of each phratry in the
yaa, or administrative headquarters. The *yaa*
is a large nomadic settlement made up of the
families of the highest political, religious, and
legal elders of the phratry. All the "ordinary"
Gabra people living outside the *yaa* are known

as *c'eeko*. The army was made up of the young warriors of the *c'eeko* and the military leaders of the *yaa*. It was through cooperation of the *c'eeko* and *yaa* that the peace of the Gabra was maintained. Any disputes not resolved at other levels were taken for legal action to the *yaa*, where specialists in the law were consulted.

The Gabra version of the *Gada* system of government common to all Oromo in the precolonial period is known as the *Luba*. Like *Gada*, *Luba* is composed of two opposed but complementary institutions: *Luba*, representing political power, and *Qaalluu*, representing spiritual authority. Through the *Luba* system power is democratically shared in Gabraland, and the affairs of the whole phratry are centrally controlled through the *yaa*. Also through the *yaa*, judicial disputes that cannot be resolved through the community at large are settled.

▼ MAKEUP OF THE *LUBA* ▼

The Gabra *Luba* is made up of political and judicial councilors known as *hayyuu* and *jallaaba*, who are elected by the members of the phratry. There are two *hayyuu*, one for each moiety, and a number of *jallaaba*, representing the individual clans.

In Gabraland, the *qaalluu* derive their ultimate authority from the Booran *Qaalluu*. For this reason the Gabra *qaalluu* is spelled with a small q. The position of the *qaalluu* is hereditary and is passed from father to son in certain clans.

The *hayyuu's* insignia of office is a scepter; he is known as the Holder of the Scepter (*Abba Bokkuu*). Other dignitaries living in the *yaa* are the Firestick Elder (*Abba Uchuumaa*), the Holder of the Sacred Drum (*Abba Dibbee*), and the Holder of the Sacred Horn (*Abba Magalataa*). The drum is associated with spiritual authority; the horn, like the scepter, is a symbol of political authority. The firesticks are a symbol of life, representing the existence of the whole phratry.

The *Luba* also structures the members of the phratry into a number of grades. All the male members of society pass through these grades. The three principal grades comprise those waiting to assume political power and serving as warriors, those representing political power, and those retiring from political power into spiritual elderhood. There are also two secondary grades, a pregrade of young uncircumcised children waiting to enter the cycle, and a postgrade of elderly men who have taken leave of it. All Gabra males are circumcised, and to participate in the cycle they must be married. All the males of one generation pass together through their rites of transition from one grade to another. Transition ceremonies are often delayed for sixteen years or even longer.

A transition ceremony is a very dramatic event. The participants make a mass pilgrimage to a ceremonial site associated with the shrines of the ancestors. Members of the phratry make the trek together, with large herds of livestock needed for sacrifice. This pilgrimage is called a *Jilla*, from the Oromo word for "feast" or ritual "celebration." The last pilgrimage was held in Gabraland in 1986.

Like all aspects of Gabra culture, the time of the *Jilla* is determined by the calendar.▲

Sequence of a Gabra marriage. The groom has his head shaved, dons nuptial clothes, and participates in the building of the couple's new hut. The hut is then blessed, and a fire is lit.

chapter

4

THE GABRA CONCEPT OF TIME

FOR THE OROMO, TIME IS THE ORIGIN AND THE essence of all things. Number is the shape that time takes. All things, including ideas, come into being and pass away according to the laws of time and numbers.

The Oromo system of measuring and recording time is known as *ayyaana*. It regulates economic, social, and ritual life. It is also through this system that history is recorded and that major political, social, and ecological events are remembered. The Oromo did not need to write their history. It was memorized by the oral historians, known as *jaarsa argaa d'aggeetii*, meaning "elders who have seen and heard."

For the Oromo, time is a cycle that can be divided into segments or units. All Oromo have two types of calendars, a lunar calendar based on the twelve months of the year and a solar

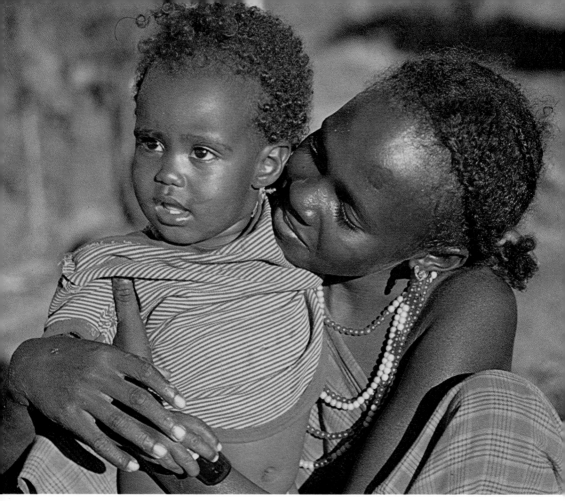

An elder sister takes care of her younger brother.

calendar based on the 365 days of the year.
Because of Islamic influence on the lowland
Gabra, their version of recording these units
differs from the Booran system.

The basic unit of time measurement is the
day (*ayyaana*). Seven days form a week.

The month is based on the pattern of the
moon. The word for month is *jiia,* meaning
"moon." The month begins when the new moon
is sighted. It is divided into two halves, fifteen
days of lightness or brightness and fifteen days

THE DAYS OF THE WEEK

In Gabra, the day begins at sunset; each evening marks the beginning of a new day. The parts of the day are distinguished by the position of the sun and the particular herding activity associated with the time: when the animals are taken to pasture in the morning, when the animals take shelter from the sun at midday, when the animals "face the sun" and begin the journey back to camp in the evening, and when they enter their enclosures for the night. Day and night are a never-ending cycle.

Days combine to form the next cycle, the week (*torbaan*, from the word for the number seven). Beginning with Friday, the most important day of the week for the Gabra, the names are:

gumaata	Friday "day of hymns" or "day of the *d'abbeelaa* elders"
sabdi	Saturday "day of cattle"
ahada	Sunday "day of camels"
alsinina	Monday "day of goats"
talassa	Tuesday "day of the hyena"
arba	Wednesday "day of the elephant"
kamisa	Thursday

People are named according to the day of the week on which they are born. They always bear two names, their "ordinary" name and their "week day" name. Some days are associated with good luck and other days with bad luck. Before any major decision is made, the proper time of day and of the week must be observed. For example, all journeys, including the movement of a settlement with its animals to a new site, must be undertaken on the correct day if its outcome is to be successful. If there is any doubt, the time-reckoning expert or *ayyaantu* is consulted.

of darkness, corresponding to the waxing and waning phases of the moon. In northern Kenya, where the skies are clear and sharp, it is quite easy to follow the course of the moon across the night sky as it sets later and later each day and then finally disappears over the horizon.

The birth (*baatii*) of the new moon is celebrated. In the morning, the head of the household applies small balls of myrrh or gum resin to the foreheads of the members of the family, and a special song is sung in praise of the moon.

In Gabra, six months of the year are lucky. During these months *sorio,* "sacrifice" for peace and prosperity, are made, and important social activities such as marriages and rites for the dead are performed. The lunar calendar forms the basis of the ritual calendar.

▼ MARKING THE YEARS ▼

The short rainy season is marked by the new year feast of *almado.* During this festival, a sort of festival of lights, fires are built and ceremonies performed for purification and peace. The *almado* rites take place over several weeks and are celebrated all over Gabraland. The name for "year" is *ganna,* which is also the name for "season," and especially the most important season, the long rainy season.

In Gabraland, each year is part of a larger cycle of time, the seven-year cycle, modeled on

The passage of time is central to the cultural life of the Gabra.

the seven-day week. Each year in this cycle is therefore given a week-day name. Thus 1994 was the Gabra Saturday Year, and 1995 is their Sunday Year. Just as weeks repeat themselves, so years also repeat themselves, and through them history is recorded. Each year is associated with some major historical or climatic event. These cycles of time and their corresponding events are

43

memorized by the oral historians. Through this cyclical record of history, the oral historians are also able to predict future cyclical events such as droughts.

The passage of time is a very important feature of Gabra life, and everything forms part of its cyclical nature: people, activities, and events.▲

chapter

5

SOCIAL CHANGE AND DEVELOPMENT

The notion of "development" in Oromo is expressed by the term *finna*. The word *finna* comes from the verb *fidu*, meaning "to hand down" and refers to the rich cultural heritage of the past that is passed down from generation to generation. *Finna* consists of a cycle of eight forms of growth.

According to the Oromo view, the universe is filled with energy. This creative and fertile flow of energy that runs through all things provides the impulse for growth. When the conditions are right, it brings about the prosperous development of man (*finna namaa*), the multiplication of stock (*finna horii*), the fruitfulness of the land (*finna lafaa*), and good fortunes of the time (*finna baraa*), and it allows the cultural traditions to flourish (*finna durii*). Peace (*nagaya*) is an essential component of this process, and the Gabra strive to maintain social peace by sacrificing and praying to *Waaqa*, the Creator.

These Gabra women follow the age-old customs of their ancestors. One woman
makes a mat out of vegetable fibers. Another pounds seeds with a mortar and pestle.

Today the Gabra are one of the few remaining groups of people in the world who still follow the age-old customs of their ancestors. They have escaped some of the more harmful aspects of Western culture that were imposed upon many peoples during the colonial and postcolonial periods. However, this lack of exposure to the outside world also means that the Gabra are not prepared to face effectively the demands of a rapidly changing world. They are now caught in a difficult position: It is impossible for them to develop according to their own culture and tradition, unaffected by the outside world. Yet they have not yet developed the means to cope in that larger world.

During the last hundred years, the Gabra have gradually become disconnected from their roots and from the ties that linked them to the great Oromo nation.

▼ COLONIALISM ▼

The isolation of the Gabra in the remote regions that straddle the Ethiopian and Kenyan border is the result of deliberate policies of the colonial and postcolonial governments. These governments were trying to "divide and rule" the Oromo, who were the legitimate owners of the land.

The boundary between Kenya and Ethiopia was marked by the British in the early 1900s.

Gabra society, although changed by colonial influences, has retained many of its customs. This woman is wearing a style of hairdressing, braids, and metallic ornament that shows she is the mother of a male child.

Hairdressing among the Gabra is very elaborate. It indicates social status and beauty. The style of the girl to the left is commonly found among girls looking to marry. The women above wear the plaits and ornaments indicating motherhood.

According to some writers, this was done to prevent the Abyssinian people from moving south from Ethiopia. According to another view, however, the Abyssinians were collaborating with the British to seize Oromo land. This group, which represented a minority in Ethiopia, possessed modern firearms and had managed to overpower the majority of Oromo and destroy their traditional *Gada* and *Qaalluu* system of leadership.

During the colonial period, the *Gada* was no longer allowed to elect its political and judicial leaders, and the Oromo system of government was replaced by colonial rule. In some remote areas—such as among the Sabbo and Goona Oromo in southern Ethiopia and northern Kenya where the Gabra live—the *Gada* and *Luba* systems have managed to survive fairly

The British colonists failed to understand why the Gabra and neighboring peoples raided one another's herds. The British limited the Gabra to very small   territories to stop the raids.

intact. However, they no longer exist as political entities, but only to fulfill a religious function.

▼ LIVESTOCK RAIDING ▼

When the British colonial administrators arrived in northern Kenya in 1909, it was common for the pastoral groups in the region between Ethiopia and Kenya to raid each other's herds. Raids were a way by which nomadic pastoralists "redistributed" and recovered livestock lost through drought and epidemic. Livestock raids occur in times of ecological stress today, although now by means of more destructive weapons such as guns.

The British saw raiding as barbaric, failing to understand the nomadic lifestyle that led to it. To prevent raids, the British created "tribal grazing areas." The Booran were allowed to graze their cattle only around Mount Marsabit, and the camel-herding Gabra were limited to the territory they occupy today. The Gabra and Booran living along the Uaso Nyiro River farther south were cut off from their compatriots to the north. Trespassing on each other's territories was severely punished by the armed police patrols organized by the British. As part of the strategy of controlling the Gabra and Booran, the British confiscated their horses, which left them unable to engage in warfare.

Formation of tribal grazing areas made it

possible to organize the nomadic pastoralists so that they could be taxed. In the case of the Gabra of Kenya, the new boundaries separated the Booran and Gabaro groups of the Sabbo and Goona Oromo. These people, once part of the same Oromo moiety, now became known as separate ethnic groups. In Ethiopia, all Sabbo and Goona are called Booran. In Kenya, the British did not understand the concept of Booran and Gabaro. They considered these complementary parts of the same society as two separate "tribes." That is how the present-day Booran and Gabra got their names.

Because of these separations caused by the British, many historians have written about the Gabra as if they were a separate ethnic group. For a long time, their history as part of Oromo society was forgotten.

During the colonial period, the part of Kenya along the Ethiopian border was called the Northern Frontier District (NFD). A high level of security was maintained in this area, and nobody was allowed to enter without a permit from the colonial administration. During World War II, the NFD was the stage from which the battle between British and Italian troops in Somalia was fought. After Kenya gained independence in 1963, instability continued in the area because of the *shifta* war. The word *shifta* means "bandit" in the Ethiopian Amharic language of the

Although colonial history records the Booran and Gabra as two distinct peoples, they are both parts of a larger group, the Oromo.

OROMO PROVERBS

Namni tolaan agabe nimbeelahu.

A generous person will not go hungry. [If you help others, they will help you.]

Gobaan isa dhaabe dire.

A sharp stake stabs the person who planted it. [Evil comes back to haunt the evildoer.]

Suuta deeman, qoren suuta nama waraanti.

If a person moves slowly, the thorn pricks him lightly. [Go with care to avoid getting hurt.]

Hantuuta baarree irra taa-u, baarreef jecha dhaban.

If a mouse is sitting on a milk gourd, people will not kill the mouse for fear of breaking the gourd.

[Sometimes trying to fix a situation only makes things worse.]

Bakka feetetti daaki, daakuun naa gali.

Grind wherever you like, but bring me the flour. [It doesn't matter how you do it, just do it!]

Titsi mana bulee, qinisi ala bule.

The fly gets to sleep in the house, but the bee has to sleep outside.

[Sometimes those who deserve rewards have a harder lot in life.]

Harren gaafaan duhe, margi hinbigilin jette.

"When I die, the grass won't grow," said the donkey.

[People tend to think of themselves as more important than they really are.]

Safaraa nyaatani, hedaa galaafatu.

What is stolen while measuring is lost by giving extra at the end—The net effect is zero, nothing gained or lost. [Do not be a miser if you are going to squander your money anyway.]

Abyssinians. This was a political movement originating in Somalia to annex part of the NFD to Somalia.

▼ INDEPENDENCE ▼

Kenya gained independence from Great Britain in 1963. Up to that time there had been virtually no schools or medical facilities in the administrative towns and trading posts such as Marsabit. Following independence, the work of providing education and health services was mainly carried out by the Roman Catholic Church. The first Catholic mission and attached primary schools were established only from 1966 onward.

As a result of the *shifta* war of secession, many Gabra lost large numbers of livestock. In the past, natural disasters such as drought had troubled their land, their people, and their animals. The Gabra had evolved ways to cope with and recover from such problems. These included a highly developed social welfare system through which the rich could help the poor to recover and reestablish themselves. The *shifta* war brought a level of loss that the Gabra had never encountered. Since then they have not been able to survive the recurrent droughts and have become dependent on food aid in times of ecological stress. This has been provided mainly through the church missions and non-governmental and international agencies.

The Gabra have struggled to develop methods to cope with the problems wrought by the *shifta* war without compromising their cultural integrity.

Many Gabra families have completely lost their herds. These families have turned to agriculture and working in the larger cities nearby.

Many Gabra have now completely lost their herds. These impoverished families have had to turn to cultivating small parcels of land on Mount Marsabit or working as night watchmen in the big cities. These changes have caused a disruption in Gabra traditions.

In the last decade, the government of Kenya has begun many projects to "develop" the Gabra territory, which have mainly had a negative impact. The provision of dams, bore-holes, and other water-catchment schemes have caused environmental damage to an already fragile ecology. The communally owned pasture land in the Hurri Hills is being subdivided into plots owned by families and used for cultivating maize and beans. This change in the ownership of land has had a negative effect on the pastoral economy by changing the grazing cycle that has allowed herding to succeed in such a difficult climate.

Oil exploration was carried out in the region

Some Gabra have had to turn to wage labor in nearby towns and cities, such as Addis Ababa, to support themselves in the face of losing their herds.

by foreign prospectors in 1989. Although this is attractive to a government interested in "modernizing" its country, the drilling and digging of oil projects threaten the natural environment as well as the traditional Gabra lifestyle.

The Gabra are a resilient and dynamic people. It is hoped that they will be able to find some way of retaining their unique Oromo identity and culture in a changing world.▲

Glossary

Aba Muudaa "Father of Anointment," the Oromo priest-king.

abba warraa Head of the family.

almado New year feast celebrating the rainy season.

badda Fertile highlands.

Booran The portion of Oromo society made up of first-born sons.

c'eeko The common Gabra people who do not live in the *yaa*.

deeda A district, made up of several *olla*.

dibbe shanaan "Five drums," the five phratries of present-day Gabra.

finna The concept of growth and development in Oromo oral history.

Gabaro The portion of Oromo society made up of younger male siblings.

Gada The traditional Oromo system of government.

gammojji Hot, dry lowlands.

ganna Oromo word for both "year" and "season."

hayyuu **and** *jallaaba* Political and legal elders, councilors in the *Luba* system.

jaarsa argaa d'aggeetii "Elders who have seen and heard," Oromo oral historians.

jiia Oromo word for both "month" and "moon."

jilla Any feast celebration; pilgrimage of a phratry to celebrate the transition of a generation of young men from one age grade to the next.

Luba The Gabra version of the traditional Oromo *Gada* system.

olla Temporary collective settlement made up of *shanaaca* who are in the area for grazing.

phratries The five territorial groups of the present-day Gabra.

qaalluu Hereditary spiritual leaders.

shanaaca A nomadic group of families made up of five *soloole*.

shifta **war** In the 1960s, a political movement to annex the NFD to Somalia.

soloola Group of closely related families forming one residential unit.

Waaqa The Oromo god.

Waata Oromo hunters and gatherers.

Warra Dasse "People of the mat," name for Eastern Cushitic nomadic peoples who travel with collapsible huts.

Warra Gaallaa "People of the camel," name for the nomadic Eastern Cushitic groups who make a living by herding camels.

yaa Politico-religious headquarters in traditional Gabra society.

For Further Reading

Almagor, P.T.W., and Almagor, U. (eds.) *Age, Generation and Time*. London: C. Hurst and Company, 1978.

Cotter, George. *Proverbs and Sayings of the Oromo People of Ethiopia and Kenya, with English Translations*. Queenston, Ontario: Edwin Mellen Press, 1992.

Challenging Reading

Dahl, G. "Suffering Grass: Subsistence and Society of the Waso Borana." *Stockholm Studies in Social Anthropology*. Stockholm: University of Stockholm, 1979.

Kassam, A. "The Fox in Gabra Oral Folktales." *Kenya Past and Present*, 14:34–43, 1982.

———. "Some Gabra Animal Beliefs." *Swara* 6(4):24–27, 1983.

———. "The Waata Hunter-gatherer/Gabra Pastoralist Symbiosis: A Symbolical Interpretation." *Sugia* 7(11):189–204, 1986.

———. "The Fertile Word. The Gabra Concept of Oral Tradition." *Africa*, 56 (2): 193–209. 1986.

———. "Gabra Ritual and Seasonal Calendars," in T. Beyne (ed.), *Proceedings of the Eighth International Conference of Ethiopian Studies*. Huntingdon: Elm Publications, 1989.

Kassam, A. and Megerssa, G. "Iron and Beads: Male and Female Symbols of Creation. A study of Ornament Among Booran Oromo," in I.

Hodder (ed.), *The Meaning of Things. Material Culture and Symbolic Expression*. London: Allen and Unwin, 1989, pp. 23–31.

———. "*Aloof alollaa*: The Inside and the Outside. Booran Oromo Environmental Law and Methods of Conservation," in D. Brokensha (ed.), *A River of Blessings: Essays in Honor of Paul Baxter*. Syracuse: Maxwell School of Citizenship and Public Affairs (African Series of Foreign and Comparative Program), 1994.

———. "Symbols of the Material Life: Sticks, Self and Society in Booran Oromo," in Arnoldi, C., Geary, C. and Hardin, K.L. (eds.), *How to Do Things with Objects: Contemporary Issues in African Material Culture Studies*. Washington, DC: Smithsonian Institution.

Legesse, A. *Gada: Three Approaches to the Study of African Society*. New York: Free Press, 1973.

———. "Oromo Democracy." *Paper presented at the Fifth Annual Congress of Union of Oromo in North America*, Toronto, 1989.

Robinson, P.W. "Gabra Nomadic Pastoralism in the 19th and 20th Century Northern Kenya. Strategies for Survival ina Marginal Environment." Unpublished doctoral dissertation: Northwestern University, 1985.

Tablino, P. *I Gabbra del Kenya*. Bogna: E.M.I., 1990.

Torry, W. "Subsistence Ecology Among the Gabra: Nomads of the Kenya/Ethiopia Frontier." Doctoral dissertation: Columbia University, 1973.

Index

A

Abba Muudaa (priest-king), 25
abba olaa (nomadic village head), 32
abba warraa (head of family), 20
Africa, Horn of, 9–10
agriculturalists, 25–26
almado (new year feast), 42
ayyaana (day), 10, 39
ayyaantu (time-reckoning expert), 41

B

baati (new moon), 42
badda (highlands), 12
Barrentu, 20
Booran, 10, 20, 52
  as rulers, 24

C

calendar, Oromo, 10
calendars, lunar and solar, 39–40
camel-herders, 9
camels, 11, 15
cattle, 11, 15
c'eeko (warriors), 35
circumcision, 36
classification, based on human figure, 20
colonialism, 47–55
cooperative policy, 29
culture, "camel," 15

D

damage, environmental, 57–58

E

Eastern Cushitic language, 10
Ethiopia, 9

F

finna (development, heritage), 45

G

Gaboro (as those ruled), 22, 24, 52
Gabra, 10
Gada (Oromo system of government), 24–25, 35, 48–49
gammojji (lowlands), 12
goats, 11, 15
  as trade, 17
grade system, 36
Great Britain, 9, 47–55

H

hayyuu (councilor), 35, 36
herd, "wet," "dry," 17–18
horses, confiscation of, 51
hunter-gatherers (Waata), 25–26

J

jaarsa argaa d'ageetii (oral historian), 49
jallaabe (councilor), 35
jiia (month), 40
Jilla (feast), 37

K

Kenya, 9

L

Luba (political power), 35, 49–50

M

milk, as main food, 15

N

nagaya (peace), 45
Northern Frontier District (NFD), 52
nomadism, seasonal, 14, 18–19, 26

O

olla (nomadic settlement), 30–32
Oromo, 9, 10, 11, 20, 35
Oromoland
   division of, 47–49, 52
   five limbs of, 21–22

P

pastoralists, 25
phratries (territorial groups), 27–28, 29, 34, 35, 37
proverbs, Oromo, 54

Q

Qaalluu (political appointees), 25, 29, 35–36, 49

R

raids, livestock, 51

S

Sakuyye, 10
seniority vs. juniority, 22–23
seven-year cycle, 42–43
shanaaca (unit of more than 5), 30
sheep, 11, 15, 17
shifta (bandit) war, 52, 55
soloola (residential unit), 29, 30
Somalia, 9

T

time and numbers, laws of, 39–44

W

Waaqa (Creator), 27, 45
Waata, 10
wage labor, dependence on, 57
watering, rules governing, 34
week, days of, 41
Worra Gaallaa (people of the camel), 15–16

Y

yaa (administrative headquarters), 27, 34, 35

ABOUT THE AUTHOR

Dr. Aneesa Kassam was born in Kenya. Chance led her to the Gabra Oromo people, changing the direction of her life. Dr. Kassam completed her doctoral dissertation on the study of the Gabra Oromo folktales in 1984. She and her husband, Dr. Gemetchu Megerssa, who comes from the western part of Oromo country, have collaborated in the writing of many articles and papers on Oromo culture and oral traditions.

Dr. Kassam is currently a lecturer in anthropology at the University of Durham, England.

PHOTO CREDITS: p. 58 © AP/Wide World Photos; all other photos © CFM, Nairobi.

DESIGN: Kim Sonsky